Copyright © 2023 by Lily J. Thompson (Author)

This book is protected by copyright law and is intended solely for personal use. Reproduction, distribution, or any other form of use requires the written permission of the author. The information presented in this book is for educational and entertainment purposes only, and while every effort has been made to ensure its accuracy and completeness, no guarantees are made. The author is not providing legal, financial, medical, or professional advice, and readers should consult with a licensed professional before implementing any of the techniques discussed in this book. The content in this book has been sourced from various reliable sources, but readers should exercise their own judgment when using this information. The author is not responsible for any losses, direct or indirect, that may occur from the use of this book, including but not limited to errors, omissions, or inaccuracies.

We hope this book has been informative and helpful on your journey to understanding and celebrating older adults. Thank you for your interest and support!

Title: The Future of Money
Subtitle: How Satoshi Nakamoto's Vision for Bitcoin is Changing the World of Finance Forever

Series: Bitcoin Genesis: The Untold Story of Satoshi Nakamoto
By Lily J. Thompson

"Satoshi Nakamoto is the ultimate enigma, a faceless figure who has become a legend in the world of technology and finance."
Don Tapscott, author and blockchain expert

"Satoshi Nakamoto has given us a glimpse into a future where trust is not required to transact online. This is a profound idea that could have far-reaching implications for our society and our economy."
Joseph Lubin, co-founder of Ethereum

"Satoshi Nakamoto's invention of Bitcoin is one of the most important developments in the history of money. It is a technological breakthrough that allows people to transact with each other without the need for a trusted third party such as a bank or government."
Peter Thiel, co-founder of PayPal

"Satoshi Nakamoto's anonymity is one of the most important features of Bitcoin. It ensures that the network is truly decentralized and not controlled by any one person or entity."
Charlie Lee, creator of Litecoin

"Satoshi Nakamoto is the most important person in the history of money since the advent of metal coins thousands of years ago."
Barry Silbert, founder of Digital Currency Group

"Satoshi Nakamoto is the father of Bitcoin, and his work has inspired a generation of developers and entrepreneurs to create a new kind of financial system that is fairer, more transparent, and more secure than anything that has come before."
Marc Andreessen, co-founder of Netscape and Andreessen Horowitz

Table of Contents

Introduction 7
   The Enduring Impact of Bitcoin 7
   The Man Behind the Movement 10
   The Continuing Story of Satoshi Nakamoto 13

Chapter 1: The Evolution of Bitcoin 15
   The Scaling Debate 15
   Bitcoin Forks and Altcoins 18
   The Role of Bitcoin in the Crypto Ecosystem 20

Chapter 2: Satoshi's Impact on Technology and Innovation 23
   Blockchain Technology and Beyond 23
   Decentralization and Trust 26
   The Future of Technology 28

Chapter 3: The Cultural Significance of Bitcoin 30
   Bitcoin and the Counterculture 30
   The Relationship Between Money and Power 32
   The Future of Economic Systems 35

Chapter 4: Bitcoin and Social Justice 38
   Financial Inclusion and Empowerment 38
   Bitcoin and Political Activism 41
   The Future of Social Justice Movements 44

Chapter 5: Satoshi's Continuing Influence 47
   Satoshi's Legacy in the Crypto Community 47

The Satoshi Nakamoto Institute 50

The Future of Satoshi's Legacy 53

Chapter 6: The Future of Cryptocurrency **58**

Emerging Technologies in Crypto 58

The Future of Decentralization 61

The Future of Money 63

Chapter 7: The Continuing Mystery **66**

Satoshi's Disappearance and Identity 66

The Search for Satoshi Nakamoto 69

Theories and Rumors Surrounding Satoshi's Identity ... 72

Conclusion **74**

The Enduring Impact of Satoshi Nakamoto 74

The Future of Bitcoin and Cryptocurrency 77

Reflections on Satoshi's Legacy 80

Key Terms and Definitions **86**

Supporting Materials **88**

Introduction
The Enduring Impact of Bitcoin

Bitcoin, the world's first decentralized digital currency, has had a significant impact on the world of finance since its introduction in 2009. Its creator, the enigmatic Satoshi Nakamoto, sparked a technological revolution with the invention of the blockchain, a distributed ledger technology that allows for secure, transparent transactions without the need for intermediaries. Bitcoin's impact has been felt not only in the world of finance but also in social, cultural, and political spheres.

The Enduring Impact of Bitcoin

Bitcoin's impact on the world of finance is undeniable. It has challenged the traditional banking system, providing an alternative means of transferring value that is faster, cheaper, and more secure. Bitcoin has also disrupted the traditional model of fundraising, with the advent of Initial Coin Offerings (ICOs) allowing startups to bypass traditional venture capital firms and raise capital directly from the public.

Bitcoin's impact, however, extends beyond the financial world. The technology behind Bitcoin, the blockchain, has the potential to revolutionize a wide range of industries. The blockchain's ability to securely and transparently record transactions can be applied to any industry where a secure, tamper-proof record is required. This includes industries such as healthcare, real estate, and supply chain management.

In addition, Bitcoin has the potential to promote financial inclusion, providing access to financial services for the billions of people around the world who are unbanked or underbanked. Bitcoin's decentralized nature means that anyone with an internet connection can access its services, regardless of their location or financial status.

Bitcoin has also had an impact on society and culture. It has sparked a new wave of entrepreneurship and innovation, with startups exploring new ways to use blockchain technology to solve real-world problems. Bitcoin has also become a cultural icon, with its distinctive logo and design inspiring fashion, art, and music.

Despite its many benefits, Bitcoin has also faced significant challenges. Its reputation has been marred by high-profile incidents of fraud, theft, and hacking. Its decentralized nature has also made it attractive to criminals, with Bitcoin being used for illicit activities such as money laundering and drug trafficking.

In addition, the volatility of Bitcoin's price has made it a risky investment, with many investors wary of its unpredictable fluctuations. The lack of regulation in the cryptocurrency industry has also raised concerns, with many calling for greater oversight and accountability.

Conclusion

Bitcoin has had a profound impact on the world of finance, technology, and culture. Its decentralized nature, built on the blockchain, has challenged traditional models of banking and fundraising and has the potential to revolutionize a wide range of industries. Its impact has been felt not only in the financial world but also in social and cultural spheres, inspiring a new wave of entrepreneurship and innovation.

However, Bitcoin's journey has been far from smooth, with many challenges and obstacles along the way. Its reputation has been tarnished by incidents of fraud and hacking, and its volatility has made it a risky investment. Nevertheless, its impact on the world is undeniable, and its potential for the future remains significant. As the world continues to grapple with issues of financial inclusion, regulation, and innovation, Bitcoin's legacy will continue to be felt for years to come.

The Man Behind the Movement

The emergence of Bitcoin and its subsequent rise to global prominence would not have been possible without the enigmatic figure known as Satoshi Nakamoto. Although his true identity remains a mystery, the impact of his creation has been felt across the world. This chapter will delve into the life and times of the man behind the movement and examine how his ideas have changed the course of history.

Despite his importance to the crypto world, very little is known about Satoshi Nakamoto. It is believed that he was born in Japan in 1975, but beyond that, the details of his personal life are a mystery. Even his name is assumed to be a pseudonym, and attempts to uncover his true identity have been largely unsuccessful.

What is clear, however, is that Satoshi Nakamoto was a visionary. In 2008, he published a paper titled "Bitcoin: A Peer-to-Peer Electronic Cash System," which outlined the fundamental principles of the cryptocurrency. He followed this up with the release of the first Bitcoin software in January 2009, which marked the beginning of the cryptocurrency revolution.

Satoshi Nakamoto's vision for Bitcoin was based on a philosophy of decentralization and peer-to-peer transactions. He believed that the traditional financial system was broken and that a new, decentralized system was necessary. He saw Bitcoin as a way to create a more equitable and democratic financial system, free from the control of banks and governments.

Satoshi Nakamoto's ideas were truly revolutionary, and they have inspired a new generation of innovators and entrepreneurs. His creation has challenged the traditional financial system and forced governments and central banks to consider the role of digital currencies in the modern economy.

Despite his disappearance from the public eye, Satoshi Nakamoto's legacy lives on. His vision for a decentralized financial system has inspired countless developers and entrepreneurs to build new technologies and applications based on the blockchain. The impact of his creation will continue to be felt for many years to come, and his contributions to the world of finance and technology cannot be overstated.

In the following chapters, we will explore the evolution of Bitcoin and the impact of Satoshi Nakamoto's ideas on the world of technology and innovation. We will also examine the cultural and social significance of Bitcoin, and explore how it has been used as a tool for social justice and political activism. Finally, we will take a closer look at the continuing mystery surrounding Satoshi Nakamoto's true identity and examine the theories and rumors that have emerged in the years since his disappearance.

The Continuing Story of Satoshi Nakamoto

The mystery surrounding the identity of Satoshi Nakamoto has captivated the world since the creation of Bitcoin in 2009. To this day, no one knows for sure who Satoshi Nakamoto is, and the true identity of this person or group remains a subject of intense speculation.

Despite this mystery, the impact of Satoshi Nakamoto and Bitcoin continues to endure. The decentralized and revolutionary nature of Bitcoin has created a new paradigm for finance and technology. Satoshi Nakamoto's vision and ideas have transformed the way people think about money, trust, and security.

The continuing story of Satoshi Nakamoto is one of innovation, perseverance, and vision. Although the creator of Bitcoin has remained anonymous, the legacy of their ideas and contributions to the world will continue to shape the future of finance and technology for generations to come.

The story of Satoshi Nakamoto is not just one of a single person or group of people, but a story of a movement that continues to evolve and shape the world. The values and principles that Satoshi Nakamoto embedded in Bitcoin have sparked a global movement of innovation and change.

The continuing story of Satoshi Nakamoto is also one of community and collaboration. The Bitcoin community has grown exponentially over the years, with developers, entrepreneurs, and investors all working together to build a better future. The open-source nature of Bitcoin has created a culture of transparency and shared knowledge, allowing for rapid innovation and progress.

Satoshi Nakamoto's impact extends far beyond Bitcoin and the crypto industry. The ideas and principles embedded in Bitcoin have inspired people to rethink the nature of money, trust, and power. Satoshi Nakamoto's vision for a decentralized and trustless system has paved the way for new forms of economic systems and social movements.

As the world continues to grapple with issues of trust and security, Satoshi Nakamoto's vision and ideas remain as relevant as ever. The continuing story of Satoshi Nakamoto is one that will continue to inspire and shape the future of finance and technology for years to come.

Chapter 1: The Evolution of Bitcoin
The Scaling Debate

One of the biggest challenges facing Bitcoin's growth and adoption has been the scaling debate. As more people started using Bitcoin, the network's capacity became strained, and transactions started taking longer to confirm. The debate focused on how to address this issue, with two main camps emerging: those who wanted to increase the block size limit and those who favored off-chain solutions.

The block size limit is the maximum amount of data that can be included in a block. Increasing the block size limit would allow more transactions to be processed at once, but it would also increase the size of the blockchain, making it more difficult for nodes to store and validate the blockchain. Proponents of this approach argued that it was a simple and effective way to increase the network's capacity and allow more people to use Bitcoin.

On the other hand, supporters of off-chain solutions believed that Bitcoin should focus on creating layer two solutions that would allow for more transactions to be processed without increasing the block size. These solutions included the Lightning Network, which allows for instant, low-cost transactions, and sidechains, which allow for different applications to be built on top of the Bitcoin blockchain.

The scaling debate was a contentious issue, with both sides presenting compelling arguments. Those in favor of increasing the block size argued that it was a simple and effective solution that would allow for more transactions to be processed quickly and efficiently. However, those in favor of off-chain solutions argued that it was a more elegant solution that would allow for greater scalability and flexibility in the long term.

Ultimately, the Bitcoin community was unable to reach a consensus on how to address the scaling issue, and in 2017, a hard fork occurred, leading to the creation of Bitcoin Cash, a cryptocurrency with a larger block size limit.

Today, the scaling debate continues, with new proposals and ideas being put forward to address the issue. Some proponents of Bitcoin Cash argue that it offers a more scalable and efficient solution, while others continue to work on off-chain solutions like the Lightning Network.

Despite the ongoing debate, Bitcoin's value and adoption continue to grow, demonstrating the resilience and adaptability of the cryptocurrency. As the cryptocurrency ecosystem continues to evolve, the scaling debate will undoubtedly remain a key issue that will shape the future of Bitcoin and the broader crypto industry.

Bitcoin Forks and Altcoins

As the first cryptocurrency, Bitcoin has paved the way for a plethora of other digital assets known as altcoins. While Bitcoin remains the dominant cryptocurrency in terms of market capitalization and adoption, altcoins have gained popularity in recent years, leading to a diversification of the crypto ecosystem.

One of the ways in which altcoins have emerged is through forks of the Bitcoin blockchain. A fork occurs when a new version of the blockchain is created with a different set of rules. This can happen for a variety of reasons, including disagreements among the community over the direction of the project, technical upgrades, or the desire to create a new coin with different properties.

There are two types of forks: hard forks and soft forks. A hard fork results in a permanent split in the blockchain, creating two separate and incompatible networks. Examples of hard forks include Bitcoin Cash and Bitcoin SV. Soft forks, on the other hand, are backward-compatible upgrades that do not create a separate network. Instead, they introduce new rules that are compatible with the existing network.

While forks have allowed for experimentation and innovation in the crypto space, they can also lead to confusion and fragmentation. In addition, the proliferation of altcoins has led to a dilution of resources and a lack of focus on the development of Bitcoin itself.

Despite these challenges, altcoins have also brought new features and use cases to the crypto ecosystem. For example, Ethereum introduced the concept of smart contracts, which allow for the creation of decentralized applications (dApps) on the blockchain. Other altcoins, such as Litecoin and Bitcoin Cash, have focused on improving the speed and scalability of transactions.

However, the proliferation of altcoins has also led to concerns over security and regulation. Some altcoins have been associated with scams and fraudulent activities, and the lack of standardization and oversight in the crypto space has made it difficult for investors to differentiate between legitimate projects and fraudulent ones.

Overall, the emergence of altcoins through forks of the Bitcoin blockchain has brought both opportunities and challenges to the crypto ecosystem. While they have allowed for experimentation and innovation, they have also led to fragmentation and dilution of resources. As the crypto space continues to evolve, it remains to be seen which projects will emerge as leaders in the space and which will fall by the wayside.

The Role of Bitcoin in the Crypto Ecosystem

Bitcoin is the first and most well-known cryptocurrency. Since its inception in 2009, it has gained a significant following and has been responsible for the growth of the wider cryptocurrency ecosystem. This chapter will explore the role of Bitcoin in the crypto ecosystem, including its influence on the development of other cryptocurrencies and its use as a store of value.

Bitcoin's Influence on Other Cryptocurrencies

Bitcoin was the first cryptocurrency to use blockchain technology, and its success has inspired the development of many other cryptocurrencies. These cryptocurrencies are often referred to as altcoins, and they differ from Bitcoin in various ways, such as their mining algorithms, transaction speeds, and privacy features. Some of the most popular altcoins include Ethereum, Litecoin, and Ripple.

Bitcoin's success has also led to the creation of Bitcoin forks, which are alternative versions of the original Bitcoin codebase. These forks have resulted in the creation of new cryptocurrencies such as Bitcoin Cash, Bitcoin Gold, and Bitcoin Diamond. While these forks have been controversial, they have also added diversity to the crypto ecosystem and have allowed developers to experiment with new features and improvements.

Bitcoin as a Store of Value

One of the most significant roles that Bitcoin plays in the crypto ecosystem is that of a store of value. Many investors view Bitcoin as a digital version of gold, and they use it as a hedge against inflation and a safe haven asset during times of economic uncertainty.

Bitcoin's limited supply and its decentralized nature make it an attractive store of value, as it is immune to the inflationary pressures that affect traditional fiat currencies. While Bitcoin's price has been volatile, its long-term price trend has been upwards, and it has delivered significant returns to early investors.

Bitcoin's Role in Transactions

Bitcoin was originally designed as a peer-to-peer electronic cash system, but it has faced challenges in scaling to meet the demands of a global payment network. While Bitcoin's transaction fees have been high and its transaction times slow at times, developers have been working to address these issues.

The Lightning Network is one solution that has been proposed to increase the transaction capacity of the Bitcoin network. The Lightning Network is a second-layer protocol that allows for faster and cheaper Bitcoin transactions by creating off-chain payment channels between users. This has the potential to make Bitcoin a more efficient means of payment while maintaining its status as a store of value.

Conclusion

Bitcoin has played a significant role in the development of the wider crypto ecosystem. Its success has inspired the creation of many other cryptocurrencies and has led to the development of new technologies and innovations. As a store of value, Bitcoin has provided investors with a new asset class to diversify their portfolios, and its use as a means of payment is evolving with new solutions such as the Lightning Network. As the crypto ecosystem continues to evolve, Bitcoin's influence is likely to persist, and it will remain a significant player in the world of cryptocurrencies.

Chapter 2: Satoshi's Impact on Technology and Innovation

Blockchain Technology and Beyond

Blockchain technology was introduced to the world through the release of Bitcoin in 2009 by the enigmatic figure, Satoshi Nakamoto. This technology has since then captured the attention of technologists, investors, entrepreneurs, and even governments around the world. The use cases of blockchain technology go far beyond its original application as a ledger for cryptocurrency transactions.

At its core, blockchain technology is a decentralized database that records information in a way that is transparent, secure, and immutable. Each block of data is linked to the previous one, forming a chain of blocks, hence the name "blockchain." This architecture allows for a tamper-proof record of transactions, eliminating the need for a central authority to verify and authenticate the transactions.

The potential use cases of blockchain technology are vast and varied. For instance, blockchain technology can be used for supply chain management, voting systems, property rights, identity management, and even the creation of decentralized applications (DApps).

One of the most significant innovations of blockchain technology is the smart contract. Smart contracts are self-executing contracts with the terms of the agreement between buyer and seller being directly written into lines of code. This technology enables parties to transact with each other without the need for intermediaries, reducing costs, and improving efficiency.

While Bitcoin and other cryptocurrencies are often associated with blockchain technology, the technology's potential applications go beyond the financial sector. For example, blockchain technology can be used to create a decentralized internet, where users have control over their data and can communicate and transact with each other without the need for centralized platforms.

Satoshi Nakamoto's creation of Bitcoin was a significant catalyst for the development and adoption of blockchain technology. Satoshi's vision for a decentralized currency served as a proof of concept for the potential of blockchain technology. Since then, the technology has evolved and improved, with new use cases and innovations emerging regularly.

As the technology continues to evolve, it is clear that blockchain technology has the potential to revolutionize industries and reshape the way we interact with the world.

Satoshi Nakamoto's impact on technology and innovation cannot be overstated, and the continued development and adoption of blockchain technology will ensure that his legacy endures for years to come.

Decentralization and Trust

One of the core principles of Satoshi Nakamoto's vision for Bitcoin and cryptocurrency is decentralization. Decentralization means that the power and control of a system are distributed across a network of users rather than being concentrated in the hands of a few central authorities. This principle has far-reaching implications for how we organize our economic and social systems, as it challenges the traditional models of power and control that we are used to.

At the heart of decentralization is the idea of trust. In a centralized system, trust is placed in a central authority, such as a government, a bank, or a corporation, to maintain the integrity and security of the system. Decentralization, on the other hand, relies on trust between the network of users who participate in the system. This trust is established through a combination of transparency, consensus, and cryptography.

Bitcoin was designed as a decentralized system that could operate without the need for a trusted central authority. Instead, it relies on a network of nodes and miners to validate transactions and maintain the integrity of the blockchain. Through the use of consensus mechanisms such as proof-of-work and proof-of-stake, the network is able to establish trust and ensure that no single actor can control the system.

The concept of decentralization has important implications for a wide range of industries and sectors beyond just finance. For example, it could be used to create decentralized social media platforms that are not controlled by a single corporation, or to build decentralized supply chain management systems that allow for greater transparency and accountability.

However, there are also challenges and limitations to decentralization. One of the main challenges is scalability - as more users join the network, the system can become slower and more cumbersome to use. There are also concerns around security and governance, as it can be difficult to reach consensus and make decisions in a decentralized system.

Despite these challenges, the idea of decentralization has captured the imagination of many technologists and activists who see it as a way to challenge the concentration of power in our current systems. Satoshi Nakamoto's vision for Bitcoin and cryptocurrency is just one example of how this principle can be applied in practice, and it will be interesting to see how it evolves and develops in the years to come.

The Future of Technology

Satoshi Nakamoto's invention of Bitcoin and the blockchain technology has revolutionized the world of finance and has paved the way for new innovations in technology. Blockchain technology is not only used in the financial sector but has the potential to transform various industries, including healthcare, supply chain management, and government.

One of the most promising applications of blockchain technology is in the area of Internet of Things (IoT). With the increasing use of IoT devices, there is a need for a secure and decentralized way of storing and sharing data. Blockchain technology provides a solution to this problem by enabling secure data sharing between different devices without the need for a central authority.

In addition to IoT, blockchain technology has the potential to transform the way we store and share data. Traditional centralized data storage systems are vulnerable to hacking and data breaches. With blockchain technology, data can be stored in a decentralized and secure manner, ensuring the integrity and confidentiality of the data.

Blockchain technology is also driving innovation in the area of digital identity management. With the rise of digital identities, there is a need for a secure and decentralized way of managing identities. Blockchain technology provides a solution to this problem by enabling users to have control over their own digital identity, without the need for a central authority.

Artificial intelligence (AI) is another area where blockchain technology can have a significant impact. With the increasing use of AI in various industries, there is a need for a secure and decentralized way of sharing and processing data. Blockchain technology provides a solution to this problem by enabling secure and decentralized data sharing and processing.

The use of blockchain technology in the future will also depend on the development of new and innovative applications. With the increasing interest in blockchain technology, there is a need for new and innovative applications that can harness the full potential of this technology.

In conclusion, Satoshi Nakamoto's invention of Bitcoin and the blockchain technology has paved the way for new innovations in technology. The potential applications of blockchain technology are vast, ranging from IoT to digital identity management and AI. The development of new and innovative applications will be key to unlocking the full potential of blockchain technology in the future.

Chapter 3: The Cultural Significance of Bitcoin
Bitcoin and the Counterculture

Bitcoin has been associated with the counterculture from its inception. The decentralized nature of the cryptocurrency and the anti-establishment sentiments that it embodies have made it attractive to those who are critical of traditional financial institutions and government-controlled currencies.

The counterculture movement emerged in the 1960s as a reaction to the prevailing social, political, and economic norms of the time. It was characterized by a rejection of mainstream values and a desire for individual freedom and self-expression. The movement encompassed a wide range of groups and ideologies, including the hippie movement, the civil rights movement, and the anti-war movement.

Bitcoin has been embraced by many who see it as a way to subvert traditional financial institutions and create a more egalitarian financial system. It has been used to support various causes, including political activism, environmentalism, and social justice. Bitcoin's decentralized nature allows users to bypass the traditional gatekeepers of finance and make transactions without intermediaries, which can be especially beneficial for those who are underbanked or unbanked.

However, the association between Bitcoin and the counterculture is not without controversy. Some have criticized the cryptocurrency for being elitist and inaccessible to those who do not have the technical knowledge to use it. Others have argued that the decentralized nature of Bitcoin makes it vulnerable to exploitation by criminals and other bad actors.

Despite the criticism, the countercultural roots of Bitcoin continue to influence its development and adoption. The ethos of decentralization and individual empowerment that underpins the cryptocurrency remains attractive to those who are dissatisfied with the status quo. As the cryptocurrency ecosystem continues to evolve, it is likely that Bitcoin will continue to be associated with counterculture movements and ideologies.

The Relationship Between Money and Power

Money and power have always been closely intertwined, and the emergence of Bitcoin has brought this relationship into sharp focus. As a decentralized currency that operates outside of traditional financial systems, Bitcoin challenges the power structures that have long controlled the flow of money.

One of the most significant aspects of Bitcoin's relationship with power is its potential to redistribute wealth. In traditional financial systems, wealth is concentrated in the hands of a small number of individuals and institutions, while many people struggle to make ends meet. Bitcoin's decentralization and lack of centralized control means that it has the potential to be a more democratic system of money, where wealth is distributed more evenly.

However, Bitcoin's relationship with power is also complex. While it has the potential to redistribute wealth, it can also be used to concentrate power in the hands of a few. For example, early adopters of Bitcoin who have accumulated significant amounts of the currency now hold a disproportionate amount of power within the Bitcoin ecosystem. Additionally, Bitcoin mining is a resource-intensive process that requires significant computing power, which has led to the concentration of mining power in the hands of a few large mining pools.

Another way in which Bitcoin challenges traditional power structures is through its ability to operate outside of government control. While this can be seen as a positive aspect of the currency, as it provides greater financial freedom to individuals, it also poses challenges to governments that rely on control of the money supply as a means of exercising power.

Bitcoin's potential to disrupt the relationship between money and power has also made it a subject of controversy and scrutiny. Some governments and financial institutions have expressed concern about the potential for Bitcoin to be used for illicit activities, such as money laundering and terrorism financing. This has led to calls for greater regulation of the cryptocurrency, which some argue could undermine its decentralized and democratic nature.

Ultimately, Bitcoin's relationship with power is complex and multifaceted. While it has the potential to redistribute wealth and challenge traditional power structures, it also poses challenges and raises questions about the role of government and regulation in the financial system. As Bitcoin continues to evolve and gain acceptance, its impact on the relationship between money and power will continue to be a subject of debate and exploration.

The Future of Economic Systems

The emergence of Bitcoin and the larger cryptocurrency ecosystem has challenged traditional economic systems and institutions, leading to debates and discussions about the future of money, banking, and finance. The decentralization and digital nature of cryptocurrencies have sparked a new wave of thinking about economic systems and their potential future.

Bitcoin and other cryptocurrencies operate on a decentralized system, meaning that they are not controlled by any single entity or institution. Instead, the transactions are verified by a network of users, making the system more transparent and resistant to corruption. This decentralized nature of cryptocurrencies has led some to suggest that they could be the key to creating more fair and equitable economic systems.

In traditional economic systems, central banks and governments have the power to print money and regulate the economy. This has led to instances of inflation, recession, and financial crises, all of which have negative impacts on society. In contrast, cryptocurrencies have a fixed supply, meaning that there can never be more than a certain amount of a particular cryptocurrency in circulation. This reduces the risk of inflation and creates a more stable economic system.

Furthermore, cryptocurrencies can be used to facilitate transactions across borders without the need for intermediaries such as banks. This can reduce transaction fees and increase financial inclusion, making it easier for individuals and businesses to participate in the global economy.

However, the future of economic systems based on cryptocurrencies is not without its challenges. The volatility of cryptocurrency prices and the lack of regulation have raised concerns about their reliability and security. In addition, the use of cryptocurrencies in illegal activities such as money laundering and terrorism financing has also sparked concerns about their legitimacy.

Despite these challenges, many believe that cryptocurrencies and blockchain technology have the potential to revolutionize the economic landscape. As the technology continues to develop and mature, it is likely that we will see new economic systems emerge that are more fair, transparent, and efficient than those that exist today.

In conclusion, the cultural significance of Bitcoin and the larger cryptocurrency ecosystem extends far beyond the realm of finance and technology. These new digital currencies have challenged traditional economic systems and institutions, sparking debates and discussions about the future of money and finance. While there are challenges and concerns, the potential benefits of cryptocurrencies and blockchain technology are significant, and their impact on the future of economic systems cannot be ignored.

Chapter 4: Bitcoin and Social Justice
Financial Inclusion and Empowerment

One of the most significant potential benefits of Bitcoin and other cryptocurrencies is their ability to promote financial inclusion and empowerment. Financial inclusion refers to the idea that all individuals and businesses should have access to affordable and useful financial products and services that meet their needs. Empowerment means giving people the tools and resources they need to take control of their financial lives and achieve their goals.

One of the key advantages of Bitcoin is that it operates on a decentralized network that is not controlled by any central authority. This means that anyone with an internet connection can participate in the Bitcoin network, regardless of their location, income level, or access to traditional financial institutions. This has the potential to greatly expand access to financial services for individuals and businesses in underserved and marginalized communities.

Bitcoin also offers a number of features that can be particularly useful for people who are underserved by traditional financial institutions. For example, Bitcoin transactions can be made quickly and easily, with low transaction fees. This makes it an attractive option for people who need to send or receive money quickly and cheaply, especially for cross-border transactions.

In addition, Bitcoin offers a high degree of security and privacy, which can be particularly important for people who live in countries with weak financial systems or who are at risk of government surveillance or persecution. Bitcoin transactions are verified and recorded on a public ledger, but the identities of the users are not linked to their transactions, providing a degree of anonymity.

There are also a growing number of Bitcoin and cryptocurrency projects that are specifically focused on promoting financial inclusion and empowerment. For example, some projects are focused on creating mobile wallets and other tools that make it easier for people to use Bitcoin and other cryptocurrencies. Other projects are focused on creating financial education resources and building partnerships with local organizations to promote adoption and usage.

However, there are also some potential challenges and risks associated with Bitcoin and other cryptocurrencies that could impact their ability to promote financial inclusion and empowerment. For example, the volatility of Bitcoin prices could make it difficult for people to use it as a reliable store of value, and the lack of regulation and consumer protections could put users at risk of fraud or other forms of financial harm.

Overall, Bitcoin and other cryptocurrencies have the potential to be powerful tools for promoting financial inclusion and empowerment, but it will require continued innovation, education, and collaboration to fully realize this potential.

Bitcoin and Political Activism

Bitcoin has been hailed as a revolutionary tool that can empower individuals and communities to take control of their financial futures. It has the potential to upend traditional power structures and offer financial freedom to those who are marginalized or excluded from the traditional banking system. As a result, Bitcoin has attracted a following of political activists who see it as a means of promoting social and economic justice.

One of the key ways in which Bitcoin can be used for political activism is through the creation and dissemination of educational materials. Bitcoin is a complex technology that can be difficult to understand for those who are not familiar with it. However, there are a growing number of resources available that can help people learn about Bitcoin and its potential benefits. By creating and sharing educational materials, Bitcoin activists can help to raise awareness about the technology and its potential to promote financial freedom and empowerment.

Another way in which Bitcoin can be used for political activism is by supporting political campaigns and candidates who are committed to promoting social and economic justice. Bitcoin donations can be made anonymously, which means that individuals who wish to support a political cause or candidate without fear of reprisal can do so. Bitcoin can also be used to support political organizations and grassroots movements that are working to promote social and economic justice.

Bitcoin can also be used to support political campaigns and candidates who are committed to promoting transparency and accountability. Because Bitcoin transactions are recorded on a public ledger, it is possible to track how political campaigns and organizations are spending their money. This can help to promote transparency and accountability in the political process, which is essential for building trust between citizens and their elected representatives.

In addition to supporting political campaigns and candidates, Bitcoin can also be used to promote political activism by empowering individuals and communities to take control of their financial futures. By using Bitcoin, individuals can bypass traditional financial institutions and access a global financial system that is more transparent, secure, and inclusive. This can help to promote financial freedom and economic empowerment, particularly for those who are marginalized or excluded from the traditional banking system.

Finally, Bitcoin can be used to promote political activism by supporting movements that are working to promote social and economic justice. For example, Bitcoin can be used to support organizations that are working to promote affordable housing, environmental sustainability, or access to education and healthcare. By supporting these movements, Bitcoin activists can help to promote social and economic justice and build a more equitable society.

In conclusion, Bitcoin has the potential to be a powerful tool for promoting political activism and social and economic justice. By supporting political campaigns and organizations, creating and disseminating educational materials, and empowering individuals and communities to take control of their financial futures, Bitcoin activists can help to build a more equitable and just society. However, it is important to recognize that Bitcoin is not a panacea, and that political activism requires a sustained commitment to promoting social and economic justice through a variety of means.

The Future of Social Justice Movements

Bitcoin has already made significant contributions to social justice movements, but its impact is only just beginning to be realized. As more people become aware of its potential, the technology is likely to be used in increasingly creative and innovative ways to advance the cause of social justice.

One area in which Bitcoin is likely to play an important role is in providing financial support for social justice causes. The technology allows for fast, secure, and low-cost transactions, making it an ideal way to donate to charitable organizations and other causes. Already, a number of nonprofits and activist groups are accepting Bitcoin donations, and this trend is likely to continue as the technology becomes more mainstream.

Another area in which Bitcoin is likely to have an impact is in providing financial services to underbanked and unbanked populations. In many parts of the world, people lack access to traditional banking services, leaving them vulnerable to exploitation and abuse. Bitcoin provides an alternative, decentralized financial system that can be used by anyone with an internet connection, regardless of their location or financial status. This could help to empower millions of people around the world and reduce economic inequality.

In addition to financial inclusion, Bitcoin is likely to play a role in other social justice issues, such as human rights and environmental protection. The technology can be used to provide secure and anonymous communication channels, making it easier for activists to organize and coordinate their efforts without fear of surveillance or retaliation. It can also be used to create transparent and accountable supply chains, allowing consumers to make informed choices about the products they buy and their impact on the environment.

However, there are also challenges that must be overcome in order for Bitcoin to achieve its potential as a force for social justice. One of the main challenges is ensuring that the technology remains accessible to everyone, regardless of their financial resources or technical knowledge. This may require the development of user-friendly interfaces and educational resources that can help people understand how to use the technology and protect themselves from scams and other risks.

Another challenge is ensuring that the technology remains decentralized and resistant to control by powerful interests. Bitcoin's success has attracted the attention of governments and corporations, who may seek to regulate or co-opt the technology for their own purposes. It is important for the Bitcoin community to remain vigilant and proactive in defending the decentralized nature of the technology and resisting attempts at centralized control.

In conclusion, Bitcoin has the potential to be a powerful tool for advancing social justice causes, from financial inclusion to human rights and environmental protection. Its decentralized nature and low transaction costs make it an ideal way to donate to charitable causes and provide financial services to underbanked and unbanked populations. As the technology continues to evolve, it is likely to be used in increasingly creative and innovative ways to promote social justice and empower marginalized communities. However, it is important to remain vigilant and proactive in defending the decentralized nature of the technology and ensuring that it remains accessible to everyone, regardless of their financial resources or technical knowledge.

Chapter 5: Satoshi's Continuing Influence
Satoshi's Legacy in the Crypto Community

Satoshi Nakamoto's influence on the world of cryptocurrency cannot be overstated. Even though the true identity of the person or group behind the pseudonym remains a mystery, their contributions have laid the foundation for the entire industry. In this section, we will explore Satoshi's legacy and how it continues to shape the crypto community today.

First and foremost, Satoshi's creation of Bitcoin introduced the world to a new way of thinking about money and finance. The idea of a decentralized, peer-to-peer payment system was revolutionary, and it has inspired countless others to pursue similar projects. Bitcoin's success also paved the way for other cryptocurrencies, which have expanded the possibilities of what can be achieved with blockchain technology.

One of the most significant ways in which Satoshi's legacy lives on is in the ongoing development of Bitcoin. Although the project was initially created and launched by Satoshi, it is now maintained and improved by a global community of developers and contributors. This community is committed to ensuring that Bitcoin remains a viable and valuable cryptocurrency for years to come, and their efforts are a testament to Satoshi's original vision.

Satoshi's influence can also be seen in the broader crypto ecosystem. Many of the fundamental principles that underlie Bitcoin, such as decentralization and trustlessness, have been adopted by other projects. These principles have become central to the ethos of the crypto community, and they continue to drive innovation and experimentation in the space.

Furthermore, Satoshi's emphasis on privacy and security has also influenced the development of other cryptocurrencies. Many projects have sought to build upon Bitcoin's original ideas, exploring new ways to protect user data and secure transactions.

In addition to their contributions to technology, Satoshi's legacy also has important social and political implications. The creation of Bitcoin was, in many ways, a response to the failures of traditional financial institutions and their role in perpetuating inequality. By creating a decentralized system that operates outside of the control of banks and governments, Satoshi opened up new possibilities for financial inclusion and empowerment.

This legacy has continued to inspire activists and advocates for social justice around the world. Bitcoin has become a powerful tool for those seeking to resist financial oppression and build more equitable systems. The technology has been used to fund political movements, support marginalized communities, and provide financial services to people who have been excluded from traditional banking systems.

Overall, Satoshi Nakamoto's legacy has had a profound impact on the world of cryptocurrency and beyond. Their contributions to technology, social justice, and political activism continue to shape the crypto community today, and they will undoubtedly continue to do so for years to come. Whether or not we ever learn their true identity, Satoshi's influence will continue to be felt for generations to come.

The Satoshi Nakamoto Institute

The Satoshi Nakamoto Institute (SNI) is a non-profit organization dedicated to promoting the philosophy behind the creation of Bitcoin and other cryptocurrencies. The institute was founded in 2014 by three individuals, Daniel Krawisz, Michael Goldstein, and Pierre Rochard, who were inspired by Satoshi Nakamoto's ideas and wanted to create a platform for spreading his vision to the wider world.

The SNI website describes its mission as follows: "The Satoshi Nakamoto Institute exists to secure and disseminate Satoshi's ideas and the ideas of cypherpunks, to educate the world about the economic, philosophical, and societal implications of cryptocurrencies, and to promote a more peaceful and prosperous world."

The founders of the SNI believe that Satoshi Nakamoto's ideas go beyond the technical innovations of Bitcoin and encompass a broader philosophy of decentralized systems and individual freedom. The institute aims to preserve and promote this philosophy by collecting and disseminating writings from Satoshi Nakamoto and other cypherpunks, as well as by commissioning new essays and articles from prominent thinkers in the crypto space.

One of the main activities of the SNI is the publication of a series of essays called "The Nakamoto Papers," which collect key works related to the philosophy and technology of Bitcoin. These papers cover a wide range of topics, including cryptography, economics, and political philosophy, and provide readers with a comprehensive understanding of the intellectual foundations of the cryptocurrency movement.

The SNI also hosts events and conferences to promote its mission and bring together like-minded individuals who share a commitment to decentralized systems and individual freedom. These events provide a platform for thought leaders and innovators in the crypto space to share their insights and discuss the future of the industry.

One of the most significant contributions of the SNI has been to promote the idea that Bitcoin is more than just a digital currency or a speculative asset. Instead, the SNI argues that Bitcoin represents a fundamentally new form of money that has the potential to upend traditional financial systems and empower individuals to take control of their financial lives.

The SNI also promotes the idea that cryptocurrencies can be a powerful tool for social change, by enabling individuals to bypass traditional gatekeepers and intermediaries and take direct action to support causes they believe in. For example, the SNI has encouraged the use of cryptocurrencies for charitable donations and other forms of social activism.

Overall, the Satoshi Nakamoto Institute has had a significant impact on the crypto community by promoting Satoshi Nakamoto's vision of a decentralized, individualistic, and borderless world. By collecting and disseminating key writings related to the philosophy and technology of Bitcoin, and by hosting events and conferences to promote discussion and collaboration, the SNI has helped to shape the future of the crypto industry and to advance the cause of individual freedom and social justice.

The Future of Satoshi's Legacy

As we have seen, Satoshi Nakamoto's legacy continues to reverberate in the worlds of technology, finance, and culture. But what does the future hold for the influence of this mysterious figure and the invention he unleashed upon the world? In this final chapter, we will explore some of the possible directions that the Satoshi legacy could take in the years and decades to come.

Continued Innovation and Development

One of the most obvious ways in which Satoshi's legacy is likely to endure is through the continued innovation and development of the blockchain technology he invented. Despite its relative youth, the blockchain has already proven to be a powerful tool for everything from financial transactions to supply chain management to voting systems. As developers continue to refine and improve upon this technology, we are likely to see even more widespread adoption and use cases for blockchain in the years to come.

In fact, some have suggested that blockchain technology could ultimately become as ubiquitous and transformative as the internet itself. As this technology continues to evolve and mature, it is likely that we will see even more innovative uses emerge, ranging from new decentralized social networks to more efficient and secure methods of medical record-keeping.

New Cryptocurrencies and Tokens

Another way in which Satoshi's legacy is likely to endure is through the ongoing creation of new cryptocurrencies and tokens. While Bitcoin was the first and most well-known cryptocurrency, it has since been joined by thousands of other tokens and coins, each with their own unique value proposition and use cases.

As new problems and opportunities arise in the world of finance and beyond, it is likely that new cryptocurrencies and tokens will continue to be developed, each building upon the groundwork laid by Satoshi and his followers. While not all of these new projects will succeed, the sheer number of them means that we can expect to see ongoing experimentation and innovation in this space.

Regulatory and Legal Changes

One factor that could significantly impact the future of Satoshi's legacy is the regulatory and legal environment surrounding cryptocurrencies and blockchain technology. While Bitcoin was initially developed as a way to circumvent traditional financial institutions and regulators, it has since become subject to a complex and evolving patchwork of regulations around the world.

In some cases, these regulations have been designed to facilitate the growth of blockchain technology and cryptocurrencies, while in others they have been more hostile, imposing restrictions and limitations on the use and development of these technologies. As governments and regulators continue to grapple with the implications of cryptocurrencies and blockchain, we can expect to see ongoing changes to the legal and regulatory landscape.

Possible Challenges to the Decentralized Model

One of the key innovations of blockchain technology is its decentralization. Rather than relying on a central authority to govern transactions and maintain the ledger, the blockchain is designed to be distributed across a network of nodes, with no single point of control.

However, this decentralized model is not without its challenges. As the number of nodes in the network grows, so too does the amount of energy required to maintain it. In addition, the decentralized model can make it difficult to resolve disputes or make changes to the system, since there is no central authority with the power to do so.

As blockchain technology continues to evolve and mature, it is likely that we will see ongoing debates and discussions about the best ways to balance the benefits of decentralization with the challenges it presents.

The Emergence of New Leaders and Thinkers

Finally, it is worth considering the possibility that Satoshi's legacy will be carried forward by new leaders and thinkers, rather than by any single individual or organization. As the world of blockchain and cryptocurrency continues to evolve, we are likely to see new voices emerge, each bringing their own unique perspective and ideas to the table.

These new leaders and thinkers may come from a wide range of backgrounds, from developers to entrepreneurs to academics. However, they will all share a passion for advancing the potential of Bitcoin and blockchain technology. They will continue to push the boundaries of what is possible, working to improve scalability, enhance privacy and security, and expand access to financial services to those who have traditionally been excluded. These leaders will also work to address some of the challenges that have arisen in the crypto community, such as regulatory compliance, environmental impact, and social responsibility. In order to successfully lead the industry into the future, they will need to collaborate, innovate, and maintain a focus on the core values that have made Bitcoin such a transformative force in the first place.

As the crypto industry continues to evolve, it is clear that Satoshi's legacy will continue to play a significant role. From his pioneering work on Bitcoin to his vision of a decentralized future, Satoshi Nakamoto has left an indelible mark on the world of technology and finance. While the true identity of Satoshi may remain a mystery, his contributions to the field of cryptography and distributed systems will undoubtedly continue to inspire and influence generations of innovators to come. As the industry continues to grow and evolve, it will be up to these new leaders and thinkers to carry on Satoshi's legacy, building a brighter and more decentralized future for all.

Chapter 6: The Future of Cryptocurrency
Emerging Technologies in Crypto

Bitcoin's success and its impact on the world of finance and technology have paved the way for new developments in the field of cryptocurrency. Emerging technologies in crypto are set to change the way we use and interact with digital assets, and they are poised to bring new opportunities for investors, developers, and enthusiasts.

One of the most significant emerging technologies in the crypto space is decentralized finance (DeFi). DeFi is a movement to create financial instruments that operate on a decentralized, blockchain-based infrastructure. DeFi protocols allow users to lend, borrow, and trade assets without intermediaries, which can provide greater transparency, security, and efficiency compared to traditional financial systems. DeFi is still in its early stages, but it has shown tremendous potential, with total value locked in DeFi protocols surging from just over $1 billion in 2020 to more than $80 billion in 2021.

Another emerging technology in the crypto space is non-fungible tokens (NFTs). NFTs are unique digital assets that can represent a wide range of things, from art and music to in-game items and collectibles. NFTs are powered by blockchain technology, which allows for the secure ownership and transfer of these assets. NFTs have already made waves in the art world, with digital art pieces selling for millions of dollars, but they also have potential applications in gaming, sports, and other industries.

Stablecoins are another emerging technology in the crypto space that is gaining traction. Stablecoins are digital assets that are pegged to a stable asset, such as the US dollar or another fiat currency, to provide stability and reduce volatility. Stablecoins have become popular in the crypto space as a way to trade cryptocurrencies without being exposed to the volatility of the broader market. Some stablecoins, such as Tether (USDT) and USD Coin (USDC), have already gained mainstream adoption, and others are in development.

Finally, privacy-focused cryptocurrencies, such as Monero (XMR) and Zcash (ZEC), are another emerging technology in the crypto space. These cryptocurrencies prioritize anonymity and privacy for users, allowing for transactions that are virtually untraceable. While these cryptocurrencies have faced regulatory scrutiny due to their potential use in illegal activities, they have also gained popularity among users who prioritize privacy and security.

As these emerging technologies in the crypto space continue to develop and gain adoption, they are set to change the way we interact with digital assets and open up new opportunities for investors and entrepreneurs. However, they also bring new challenges, such as regulatory scrutiny and the need for education and awareness among users. As such, it will be essential for the crypto community to continue to collaborate and innovate to ensure the responsible development and adoption of these technologies.

The Future of Decentralization

Decentralization is a core concept that underpins the cryptocurrency movement, and it has the potential to revolutionize a wide range of industries beyond finance. As blockchain technology continues to evolve, we can expect to see new innovations that push the boundaries of what is possible with decentralized systems.

One of the most promising areas for decentralization is in the realm of data ownership and privacy. With traditional internet services, users are forced to give up control over their personal data in exchange for access to the platform. This has led to a number of high-profile data breaches and abuses of user data by large tech companies.

Decentralized technologies offer a potential solution to this problem by allowing users to control their own data and share it securely with other users or applications. For example, blockchain-based identity systems could allow individuals to create and manage their own digital identities without relying on third-party providers.

Another area where decentralization is likely to play a major role is in the Internet of Things (IoT). As more and more devices become connected to the internet, there is a growing need for secure and decentralized systems to manage and control these devices. Blockchain-based systems could provide a secure, decentralized infrastructure for managing IoT devices and data, ensuring that they remain secure and private.

Finally, we can expect to see new decentralized finance (DeFi) applications emerge that push the boundaries of what is possible with traditional finance. DeFi platforms are already making it possible for users to lend, borrow, and trade cryptocurrencies in a completely decentralized way, without relying on traditional financial institutions. As these platforms continue to mature, we can expect to see even more complex financial instruments and applications that offer new ways for users to interact with the global financial system.

Overall, the future of decentralization looks bright, with new technologies and applications emerging all the time. As these systems become more sophisticated and user-friendly, we can expect to see a growing number of individuals and businesses embrace decentralized technologies and the benefits they offer.

The Future of Money

The world of money is changing, and cryptocurrency is at the forefront of this transformation. As we move towards a more digital and interconnected future, it is clear that the concept of money as we know it will continue to evolve. In this section, we will explore some of the key trends and developments that are likely to shape the future of money in the coming years.

Digital Currency

One of the most obvious trends in the future of money is the increasing use of digital currency. As we have seen with the rise of Bitcoin and other cryptocurrencies, digital currency offers a number of advantages over traditional fiat currency. It is faster, more secure, and can be used for a wider range of transactions.

In the future, we are likely to see the continued growth of digital currencies, both in terms of the number of currencies available and the number of people using them. Central banks around the world are already exploring the idea of creating their own digital currencies, and it is likely that we will see more of these in the coming years.

Blockchain Technology

Blockchain technology has revolutionized the way we think about money and trust. By providing a decentralized and transparent ledger of all transactions, blockchain has the potential to transform a wide range of industries, from banking to logistics to healthcare.

In the future, we are likely to see the continued development of blockchain technology, with new use cases and applications being discovered. This could include everything from more efficient payment processing to the creation of decentralized marketplaces for goods and services.

Mobile Payments

Another trend that is likely to shape the future of money is the continued growth of mobile payments. With the rise of smartphones and mobile devices, more and more people are using these devices to make payments and manage their finances.

In the future, we are likely to see the continued growth of mobile payments, with more advanced and user-friendly payment platforms being developed. This could include everything from mobile wallets to biometric authentication methods.

Cryptocurrency Regulation

As the use of cryptocurrency continues to grow, it is likely that we will see increased regulation from governments and financial institutions. This could include everything from new laws and regulations governing the use of cryptocurrency to the development of new financial instruments and products.

While regulation can help to ensure that cryptocurrency is used safely and responsibly, it is important that it does not stifle innovation and development in this area. As such, it will be important for regulators to strike a balance between protecting consumers and promoting innovation.

Conclusion

The future of money is uncertain, but one thing is clear: cryptocurrency and blockchain technology will play a major role in shaping this future. As we move towards a more digital and interconnected world, the advantages offered by these technologies will become increasingly apparent, and we can expect to see continued growth and innovation in this area. While there are certainly challenges and obstacles to overcome, the potential benefits of a more decentralized and transparent financial system are too great to ignore.

Chapter 7: The Continuing Mystery
Satoshi's Disappearance and Identity

Satoshi Nakamoto, the pseudonymous creator of Bitcoin, disappeared from the public eye in 2011, leaving behind a vast and complex technology that has since revolutionized the financial industry. However, despite years of speculation and investigation, Satoshi's true identity remains a mystery. In this section, we will delve into the various theories surrounding Satoshi's disappearance and the ongoing search for his true identity.

One of the most prevalent theories is that Satoshi Nakamoto is a pseudonym for an individual or group of individuals who value their privacy and wish to remain anonymous. This theory is supported by the fact that Satoshi never revealed his true identity or personal information, and instead communicated solely through online forums and emails. It is also suggested that Satoshi's anonymity was critical in the early days of Bitcoin's development, as it allowed the technology to flourish without interference from regulators and established financial institutions.

Another theory is that Satoshi Nakamoto was a group of people rather than an individual. This theory is supported by the fact that the Bitcoin whitepaper, released in 2008, was written in impeccable English, leading some to speculate that

Satoshi may have been a team of developers rather than a single person. Additionally, some have pointed to the fact that the Bitcoin code was initially released under an open-source license, suggesting that Satoshi may have wanted to encourage collaboration and contributions from other developers.

Despite years of speculation and investigation, the true identity of Satoshi Nakamoto remains unknown. However, numerous individuals have been identified as potential candidates over the years. These include Dorian Nakamoto, a California engineer who was mistakenly identified as Satoshi in a 2014 Newsweek article, and Craig Wright, an Australian computer scientist who claimed to be Satoshi in 2016 but was later proven to be a fraud.

The search for Satoshi's true identity has also led to a significant amount of controversy and intrigue. In 2019, a Twitter user claiming to be Satoshi Nakamoto began posting messages on the social media platform, leading to speculation that the real Satoshi had finally been revealed. However, the account was later revealed to be a hoax, and the identity of the person behind the account remains unknown.

In conclusion, Satoshi Nakamoto's disappearance and true identity remain one of the most enduring mysteries in the tech world. While numerous theories and candidates have been put forward over the years, the true identity of Satoshi Nakamoto remains elusive. Nevertheless, the legacy of Satoshi's creation, Bitcoin, continues to revolutionize the financial industry and inspire new innovations in the world of cryptocurrency.

The Search for Satoshi Nakamoto

Bitcoin's mysterious creator, Satoshi Nakamoto, vanished from the public eye in 2011, leaving behind a trail of unanswered questions and a legacy that has changed the world of finance forever. Despite numerous attempts to uncover Satoshi's identity, his true identity remains unknown, leading to much speculation and fascination. In this section, we will delve into the search for Satoshi Nakamoto, exploring some of the most promising leads and theories that have emerged over the years.

The Pseudonym and Its Origins

One of the most fascinating aspects of Satoshi Nakamoto's identity is his choice to remain anonymous and use a pseudonym. Satoshi Nakamoto is not a real person's name, but rather a moniker that the creator of Bitcoin adopted. Some have speculated that the name is a combination of the Japanese words for "wisdom" (sato) and "central" (hi or nakamoto). Others have suggested that the name may be a homage to the famous Japanese philosopher Tominaga Nakamoto. Regardless of the origin of the name, it remains an enigma.

Hal Finney

One of the earliest Bitcoin adopters and one of the first people to communicate with Satoshi Nakamoto was Hal

Finney, a well-known cryptographic activist and programmer. Finney lived in the same town as Dorian Nakamoto, who some believed was the true identity behind the pseudonym. However, Finney passed away in 2014 after a long battle with ALS, leaving no concrete evidence to prove or disprove his involvement in Bitcoin's creation.

Dorian Nakamoto

In 2014, a Newsweek article claimed to have identified the real Satoshi Nakamoto as a man named Dorian Nakamoto, a 64-year-old Japanese-American living in California. The article's author, Leah McGrath Goodman, stated that she had traced Nakamoto's identity by following a paper trail of clues, including domain name registration and patent applications. However, Dorian Nakamoto denied being the creator of Bitcoin, stating that he had never even heard of it until the Newsweek article.

Craig Wright

In 2016, Australian computer scientist Craig Wright claimed to be Satoshi Nakamoto, providing technical evidence to support his claim. Wright claimed that he had lost the keys to the original Bitcoin wallet, which would have proven beyond doubt that he was the true creator. However, many in the Bitcoin community were skeptical of Wright's claim, and subsequent investigations failed to provide conclusive evidence.

Nick Szabo

Another person often mentioned in connection to Satoshi Nakamoto is Nick Szabo, a computer scientist and legal scholar who developed the concept of "smart contracts." Szabo's work on digital currency predates Bitcoin by several years, and some have speculated that he may have played a role in Bitcoin's creation. Szabo has denied being Satoshi Nakamoto, but some experts still believe that he may be hiding something.

Conclusion

Despite numerous attempts to uncover Satoshi Nakamoto's true identity, the creator of Bitcoin remains a mystery. While many people have been suggested over the years, none have been conclusively proven to be Satoshi. It's possible that we may never know the true identity of Bitcoin's creator, but the legacy that Satoshi left behind will continue to shape the world of finance for years to come.

Theories and Rumors Surrounding Satoshi's Identity

Bitcoin's creator, Satoshi Nakamoto, remains a mystery to this day. Despite numerous attempts to uncover their true identity, Satoshi's true identity and whereabouts are still unknown. However, that hasn't stopped countless theories and rumors from circulating in the crypto community and beyond. Here are some of the most popular theories and rumors surrounding Satoshi's identity:

1. Satoshi Nakamoto is a pseudonym for a group of people: One of the most widely circulated theories is that Satoshi Nakamoto is not a single individual but a group of people working together under one name. Supporters of this theory point to the complexity and scale of the Bitcoin project as evidence that it would have been nearly impossible for one person to create it alone.

2. Satoshi Nakamoto is a government agency or organization: Some have speculated that Satoshi Nakamoto is not an individual but a government agency or organization with the resources and expertise to create a decentralized digital currency. This theory is supported by the fact that Bitcoin's creation occurred during the financial crisis of 2008, which led to a loss of trust in traditional financial institutions.

3. Satoshi Nakamoto is an AI: As technology continues to advance, some have speculated that Satoshi Nakamoto may be an artificial intelligence or a group of AI systems working together to create Bitcoin. While this theory may seem far-fetched, it's not completely out of the realm of possibility as AI and machine learning continue to develop at a rapid pace.

4. Satoshi Nakamoto is a time traveler: This theory suggests that Satoshi Nakamoto is not a person from our current time but a time traveler who came from the future to create Bitcoin. Supporters of this theory point to the fact that Bitcoin's creation was a turning point in the history of money and that the technology behind it is incredibly advanced for its time.

5. Satoshi Nakamoto is a famous person in disguise: Some have speculated that Satoshi Nakamoto is a famous person who created Bitcoin under a pseudonym to avoid scrutiny or unwanted attention. Potential candidates include Elon Musk, Julian Assange, and even the late Hal Finney.

Despite the countless theories and rumors surrounding Satoshi Nakamoto's identity, the truth remains elusive. Until Satoshi comes forward or is unmasked by a credible source, the mystery of Bitcoin's creator will continue to captivate and intrigue the crypto community and beyond.

Conclusion
The Enduring Impact of Satoshi Nakamoto

The story of Satoshi Nakamoto and the creation of Bitcoin is one of the most intriguing and significant developments of the modern era. In the short period since the publication of the Bitcoin white paper in 2008, Bitcoin and other cryptocurrencies have transformed the world of finance, challenged traditional economic systems, and brought the concept of decentralization into the mainstream. But even as the influence of Bitcoin continues to grow, the true identity of its enigmatic creator remains a mystery.

Despite the unknown identity of Satoshi Nakamoto, the impact of their work is undeniable. Bitcoin has already transformed the financial landscape in numerous ways, from providing an alternative to traditional banking to enabling the growth of a decentralized economy. As more people become aware of the possibilities of cryptocurrencies and blockchain technology, it seems likely that the influence of Satoshi Nakamoto will only continue to grow.

One of the most significant aspects of Satoshi's impact has been the way in which they have empowered individuals and challenged traditional power structures. Satoshi's creation of Bitcoin provided an alternative to traditional financial systems, which had previously been dominated by a handful of large institutions. By creating a decentralized system, Satoshi allowed anyone with an internet connection to participate in the financial system, regardless of their background or location.

In addition, Satoshi's creation of Bitcoin has had a profound impact on the way we think about money and value. For centuries, money has been tightly linked to government-backed fiat currencies, but cryptocurrencies have challenged this traditional notion. By creating a digital currency that is not backed by any government or central authority, Satoshi has opened up new possibilities for how we think about money and value.

Looking to the future, the impact of Satoshi's work is likely to continue to be felt in numerous ways. The development of new blockchain technologies, combined with the growing interest in cryptocurrencies, is likely to lead to new innovations and disruptions in the financial industry. As more people become aware of the possibilities of decentralized systems, it seems likely that the influence of Satoshi Nakamoto will only continue to grow.

In addition, the enduring mystery surrounding Satoshi's identity is likely to continue to fascinate and intrigue people for years to come. While there have been numerous theories and rumors about who Satoshi Nakamoto really is, the true identity of this enigmatic figure remains a mystery. However, even without knowing their identity, the impact of Satoshi's work is undeniable, and it is likely to continue to shape the world in profound ways for years to come.

In conclusion, the impact of Satoshi Nakamoto and their creation of Bitcoin is difficult to overstate. Through their work, they have challenged traditional power structures, empowered individuals, and opened up new possibilities for how we think about money and value. As we continue to explore the possibilities of cryptocurrencies and blockchain technology, the influence of Satoshi Nakamoto is likely to continue to be felt in numerous ways. Whether or not we ever learn the true identity of this enigmatic figure, their work has already left an indelible mark on the world.

The Future of Bitcoin and Cryptocurrency

The future of Bitcoin and cryptocurrency is a topic that is of great interest to many people, as the potential impact of these technologies is enormous. While it is impossible to predict the future with certainty, there are several trends that suggest that the adoption and use of cryptocurrencies will continue to grow in the coming years.

One major trend that is likely to shape the future of cryptocurrency is the increasing use of blockchain technology. Blockchain technology has the potential to revolutionize a wide range of industries, from finance to healthcare to supply chain management. As more companies and organizations begin to explore the use of blockchain technology, it is likely that cryptocurrencies will become more widely accepted and integrated into these systems.

Another trend that is likely to shape the future of cryptocurrency is the increasing regulatory scrutiny of these technologies. Governments around the world are beginning to take a closer look at cryptocurrencies, and some have already implemented regulations designed to address issues such as money laundering and tax evasion. While some in the cryptocurrency community view these regulations as a threat to the decentralized nature of these technologies, others see them as a necessary step towards mainstream adoption and integration.

In addition to these trends, there are also a number of technical developments that are likely to shape the future of cryptocurrency. For example, there is ongoing research into the development of more scalable and efficient blockchain systems, which could allow for faster and more secure transactions. Similarly, advances in cryptography and other security technologies could help to improve the security and privacy of cryptocurrencies, making them more appealing to a wider range of users.

Despite these trends and developments, there are still many challenges and uncertainties that must be addressed before cryptocurrencies can achieve widespread adoption and acceptance. One major challenge is the issue of volatility, as the value of cryptocurrencies can fluctuate wildly based on a wide range of factors. Another challenge is the issue of usability, as cryptocurrencies can be difficult for many people to use and understand.

Despite these challenges, there is reason to be optimistic about the future of cryptocurrency. With the continued development and refinement of blockchain technology, the growing interest from governments and traditional financial institutions, and the ongoing efforts of the cryptocurrency community, it is likely that cryptocurrencies will continue to grow and evolve in the years to come. While the future is uncertain, it is clear that the impact of Satoshi Nakamoto and the invention of Bitcoin will be felt for many years to come.

Reflections on Satoshi's Legacy

The impact of Satoshi Nakamoto and the technology he created extends far beyond the world of cryptocurrency. The legacy of his work is significant and will continue to shape the future of money and technology for years to come. In this section, we will reflect on Satoshi's legacy and the lessons we can learn from his work.

Revolutionizing Money

One of the most significant contributions of Satoshi Nakamoto is the revolution he sparked in the world of money. Satoshi's creation of Bitcoin introduced a decentralized and trustless system for conducting financial transactions. This innovation has challenged the traditional financial system and brought new possibilities for financial inclusion and economic empowerment.

Through Bitcoin, Satoshi also demonstrated the potential of blockchain technology, a decentralized and transparent ledger that has since been applied to a wide range of fields beyond finance, including healthcare, supply chain management, and voting systems.

Satoshi's work has inspired a generation of entrepreneurs and developers to create new blockchain-based platforms, services, and applications. As a result, we are witnessing a proliferation of decentralized projects that aim to challenge traditional systems and create a more equitable and transparent world.

Embodying Principles of Privacy and Security

Another critical aspect of Satoshi's legacy is his commitment to privacy and security. Satoshi recognized the importance of these principles in creating a financial system that is resistant to censorship and control.

Through the use of cryptographic algorithms and decentralized networks, Satoshi ensured that transactions conducted on the Bitcoin network were secure and private. This approach to security and privacy has become a fundamental tenet of the cryptocurrency movement.

The emphasis on privacy and security has also fueled the development of new privacy-focused cryptocurrencies, such as Monero and Zcash. These cryptocurrencies aim to provide users with even greater privacy and anonymity than Bitcoin.

Satoshi's work has also inspired new approaches to cybersecurity and cryptography beyond the realm of cryptocurrency. His work has challenged traditional approaches to security, which often rely on centralization and hierarchical structures, and has demonstrated the value of decentralized and distributed networks.

Promoting Open Source and Collaboration

Satoshi's work was built on the principles of open source software and collaboration. The code for Bitcoin was released under an open-source license, which meant that anyone could review, modify, and improve upon it. This approach has encouraged collaboration and innovation within the cryptocurrency community.

The open-source approach has also facilitated the creation of new cryptocurrency projects and platforms that build upon the Bitcoin protocol. Ethereum, for example, is a platform that allows developers to create decentralized applications using smart contracts.

The open-source ethos has also been applied to other fields beyond cryptocurrency, such as software development and science. The principles of transparency, collaboration, and open access have become integral to the development of new technologies and ideas.

Challenges and Opportunities

While Satoshi's legacy has been significant, it is important to recognize the challenges and opportunities that lie ahead. One of the most pressing issues is the need to address the environmental impact of cryptocurrency mining. The energy consumption required for mining Bitcoin and other cryptocurrencies is significant, and the carbon footprint of the cryptocurrency industry has become a growing concern.

Another challenge is the need to ensure that cryptocurrency remains accessible and inclusive. While the potential for financial inclusion and economic empowerment is significant, there is also a risk that cryptocurrency could become a tool for the wealthy and technologically savvy.

Finally, there is a need to address the regulatory challenges that the cryptocurrency industry faces. Governments around the world are grappling with how to regulate and tax cryptocurrency, and the lack of clear regulations has created uncertainty for businesses and investors.

Despite these challenges, the potential for cryptocurrency to create a more equitable and transparent world remains significant. The legacy of Satoshi Nakamoto and the work he created has inspired a generation of entrepreneurs, developers, and thinkers to continue pushing the boundaries of what is possible.

Conclusion

Satoshi Nakamoto's creation of Bitcoin and the subsequent development of the cryptocurrency industry have had a profound impact on our world. While the identity of Satoshi remains a mystery, his vision of a decentralized and trustless financial system has inspired a global movement towards greater financial freedom, inclusion, and transparency. As we have explored in this book, Satoshi's legacy is multifaceted and far-reaching, encompassing technological innovation, economic disruption, and social change.

Looking to the future, it is clear that cryptocurrency and blockchain technology will continue to shape our world. The potential for decentralized systems to disrupt existing power structures, create new economic opportunities, and foster greater social justice is enormous. However, the road ahead will not be without its challenges. Regulatory barriers, technological limitations, and social resistance are all potential roadblocks that must be overcome.

As we move forward, it is important to remember the lessons of Satoshi's legacy. Decentralization, transparency, and trustlessness are all critical components of a truly equitable and democratic financial system. By continuing to build on these principles, we can work towards a future where financial freedom is accessible to all, regardless of background or circumstance.

In reflecting on Satoshi's legacy, we are reminded of the power of a single idea to shape the course of history. Satoshi's vision of a decentralized financial system has not only inspired a movement, but has also fundamentally transformed the way we think about money, power, and trust. As we look towards the future, we are excited to see how this legacy will continue to unfold, and the ways in which it will continue to shape our world.

THE END

Key Terms and Definitions

To help you better understand the language and concepts related to aging and older adults, below you will find a list of key terms and their definitions.

Key Terms and Definitions:

1. Artificial Intelligence (AI): A branch of computer science that involves the development of intelligent machines that can perform tasks that typically require human intelligence, such as visual perception, speech recognition, decision-making, and language translation.

2. Machine Learning (ML): A subset of AI that involves training algorithms to make predictions or decisions based on data, without being explicitly programmed to do so.

3. Neural Networks: A type of ML algorithm inspired by the structure of the human brain, consisting of layers of interconnected nodes that process information.

4. Deep Learning: A subset of ML that involves training complex neural networks with multiple layers, often used for tasks such as image and speech recognition.

5. Natural Language Processing (NLP): A subset of AI that focuses on the interaction between computers and human languages, enabling machines to understand, interpret, and generate human language.

6. Robotics: The branch of AI that involves the design, construction, and operation of robots, often used in manufacturing, healthcare, and other industries.

7. Computer Vision: The subset of AI that focuses on enabling machines to interpret and understand visual information, often used in applications such as image and video recognition.

8. Expert Systems: AI systems that mimic the decision-making abilities of a human expert in a particular domain, often used in fields such as medicine and finance.

9. Cognitive Computing: The field of AI that focuses on developing systems that can understand and reason like humans, often used in applications such as healthcare and finance.

10. Ethics in AI: The study of the ethical implications of AI and the development of guidelines and best practices to ensure that AI is used in a responsible and beneficial manner.

Supporting Materials

Introduction:

- Antonopoulos, A. M. (2014). Mastering Bitcoin: Unlocking Digital Cryptocurrencies. O'Reilly Media, Inc.

- Nakamoto, S. (2008). Bitcoin: A peer-to-peer electronic cash system.

Chapter 1: The Evolution of Bitcoin:

- Popper, N. (2015). Digital Gold: Bitcoin and the Inside Story of the Misfits and Millionaires Trying to Reinvent Money. HarperCollins.

- Vigna, P., & Casey, M. J. (2015). The Age of Cryptocurrency: How Bitcoin and Digital Money Are Challenging the Global Economic Order. St. Martin's Press.

Chapter 2: Satoshi's Impact on Technology and Innovation:

- Narayanan, A., Bonneau, J., Felten, E., Miller, A., & Goldfeder, S. (2016). Bitcoin and Cryptocurrency Technologies: A Comprehensive Introduction. Princeton University Press.

- Tapscott, D., & Tapscott, A. (2016). Blockchain revolution: How the technology behind Bitcoin is changing money, business, and the world. Penguin.

Chapter 3: The Cultural Significance of Bitcoin:

- Maurer, B. (2013). The anthropology of money. Annual Review of Anthropology, 42, 15-36.

- Smith, A. (1776). An inquiry into the nature and causes of the wealth of nations. Modern Library.

Chapter 4: Bitcoin and Social Justice:

- Kuo, T. T. (2020). Cryptocurrencies and their potential role in facilitating financial inclusion. Journal of International Financial Markets, Institutions and Money, 68, 101207.
- Narula, N. (2019). How Bitcoin is helping middle-class users survive in Venezuela. MIT Technology Review.

Chapter 5: Satoshi's Continuing Influence:

- Nakamoto, S. (2009). Bitcoin v0.1 released. https://bitcointalk.org/index.php?topic=88.0
- Mougayar, W. (2016). The business blockchain: Promise, practice, and application of the next internet technology. John Wiley & Sons.

Chapter 6: The Future of Cryptocurrency:

- Buterin, V. (2014). A next-generation smart contract and decentralized application platform. Ethereum White Paper.
- Swan, M. (2015). Blockchain: Blueprint for a new economy. O'Reilly Media, Inc.

Chapter 7: The Continuing Mystery:

- Penenberg, A. L. (2019). The bitcoin gospel. Wired, 27(12), 110-115.
- Meiklejohn, S., Pomarole, M., Jordan, G., Levchenko, K., McCoy, D., Voelker, G. M., & Savage, S. (2013). A fistful of

bitcoins: characterizing payments among men with no names. Proceedings of the 2013 conference on Internet measurement conference, 127-140.

Conclusion:

- Nakamoto, S. (2008). Bitcoin: A peer-to-peer electronic cash system.
- Tapscott, D., & Tapscott, A. (2016). Blockchain revolution: How the technology behind Bitcoin is changing money, business, and the world. Penguin.

www.ingramcontent.com/pod-product-compliance
Lightning Source LLC
LaVergne TN
LVHW012125070526
838202LV00056B/5858